A BOOMER'S GUIDE to AGING

SEX
drugs &
growing
OLD

Dennis M. Garvey
GERONTOLOGIST

Dennis Garvey, gerontologist, offers programs,
materials and seminars to help people improve
their understanding of aging.

For more information on Dennis' services,
e-mail: aginginsightspublishing@gmail.com

Sex, Drugs & Growing Old—A Boomer's Guide to Aging
Copyright ©2009 by Dennis Garvey.
All rights reserved.

ISBN 978-0-9840958-0-3

Library of Congress Catalog Card Number 2009907312

Printed in the United States of America

Jacket and Book Design by Granite Mountain Graphics,
Prescott, AZ • www.gmgarts.com

Back Cover Photo by Chris Marchetti
www.marchettiphoto.com

AGING
INSIGHTS
PUBLISHING™

table of contents

Introduction —————————— 1

If You Are Planning to Grow Older, This Guide Is For You!
- It's about living, not aging
- Changing demographics create changing opportunities
- We must change the world again...and we will!

Chapter 1 —————————— 7

What Do You Think About Growing Older?
- Personal images create or limit our experience of aging
- Who will you be when you are older?
  Exercise and discussion

Chapter 2 —————————— 15

What Determines Our Images of Aging?
- History of aging
- Print and electronic media influence
- What we've been taught—images of aging in children's literature

Chapter 3 —————————— 23

The Myths of Aging Revealed
- Exploding the myths of aging
- Prisoners of our own lies—examining their consequences

Chapter 4 — 33

Aging vs. Illness
- Normal age changes—what to expect and what to reject as "normal" aging
- Influences that affect how we physically age

Chapter 5 — 43

Healthy Living
- Wellness = a balance of mind, body and spirit

Chapter 6 — 51

Caring for Aging Parents
- The *Sandwich Generation*
- When will it be my turn?
- Where did the rest of the family go?
- How much is too much?
- Knowing when you are in over your head
- Finding and accepting help

Chapter 7 — 63

Retirement: It's Not What You Think It Is!
- The changing face of retirement
- Bringing meaning to this time in your life

Chapter 8 — 71

Sex: It's Not What It Used to Be!
- The importance of intimacy
- Physical changes—males / females
- Relationships

Chapter 9 ———————————— 79

Drugs and Alcohol
- Drugs: over the counter / prescription / alcohol

Chapter 10 ———————————— 85

Rock & Roll: Are We Having Fun Yet?
- Stress reduction
- Taking responsibility for your life

Chapter 11 ———————————— 93

Developing a Personal Action Plan:
***YOU* Are in Charge!**
- Take my insightful survey

Chapter 12 ———————————— 99

Next Steps: The Boomers Are Back!

About the Author ———————— 103

Now, let's get started!

Youth is the gift of nature,
but age is a work of art.

– Stanislaw Lec

This guide is dedicated to
my wife, family and many friends
whom I have leaned upon for support
while I wrote, fretted about and imagined
how this book would turn out.

The fact that you are reading this
is testament to their
support and encouragement.

Thank you all!

The ultimate goal
of this book is
to help people
move beyond their
fears of aging
into fully
appreciating
the possibilities
that await us
all as we
grow older.

introduction

If You Are Planning to Grow Older, This Guide Is For You!

It's About Living, Not Aging.

Sex, Drugs and Growing Old — A Boomer's Guide to Aging is an informative, enjoyable book that will help you gain perspective on this "growing-older-thing."

This book explores what "aging" is really about, seeing aging as a process and not a product. The ultimate goal of this book is to help people move beyond their fears of aging into fully appreciating the possibilities that await us all as we grow older.

If you are caring for aging parents or are planning to grow older yourself, this guide will dispel many of the myths about aging. These myths steal the energy we need to fully enjoy life.

"Aging isn't so bad, when you consider the alternative."
– Maurice Chevalier

How do you want to live the rest of your life? What choices do you have as you look at the next 30, 40 or 50+

1

years? Do you know that molecular biologists believe that in the absence of disease, the human body can live to 120 years or more? As I've traveled around the country leading retirement seminars, I've come to see that people are amazed to learn how long they might live. It's one thing to plan to live another 10 or 15 years beyond retirement age, like our parents did. But to be told that in the future we can expect to live past 100 years of age is often frightening. The looks on the faces of many of my seminar participants say it all: "No way! Not me!"

> *Successful aging has a lot to do with how you live your life today, your values, and what you expect from yourself and others.*

So, let me ask again: how do you want to live the rest of your life? This is a very important question. Your attitudes and knowledge about aging will have a tremendous impact on how your life will unfold. It is important to understand that successful aging is a process, not a product. Successful aging has a lot to do with how you live your life today, your values, and what you expect from yourself and others. Throughout this guide you will find that aging successfully has very little to do with how old you are chronologically. Owing to advances in modern medicine, longevity is not a trick. We can replace almost any body part—knees, hips, heart, etc. It is an acquired skill, however, to live a life of quality—a life of meaning. Our technological advances have allowed us to live longer lives. However, they also push us to live at a faster and ever faster pace.

I am concerned about two things. One, we are losing our appreciation for the process of living. If we live life in the fast lane while allowing ourselves to miss the "ride of our lives" into old age, the notion of aging may appear to be so frightening that we will not know how we got there.

Secondly, our culture offers us very negative images of aging. It does not give us a road map for the future that is worth following. The sad fact is that most of us, by an early age, have internalized these negative images of aging and on a daily basis allow them to limit our sense of who we are and what we can become.

Media's Influence

The print and electronic advertising media are more than happy to tell us what aging is all about. From their perspective, aging is about illness, forgetfulness and being wrinkled—about bladder control problems and constipation—hardly things to look forward to!

It is sad to admit, but for the most part, people who know nothing of what the aging process is truly about are the ones who cultivate our beliefs about growing older. They manipulate our images of aging, intentionally creating a climate of fear in order to sell us products we do not need: "age-defying" make-up, wrinkle treatments, plastic surgery, and so on. It makes me sad to see both men and women subject themselves to plastic surgery and its risks so their exteriors will mask their age, when in reality it is our spirit that ultimately shows the world who we really are.

> *Do you really think that as you grow older you become less of who you are and more like those popular images of aging?*

Ageism is real. The term "ageism" was originally coined by gerontologist Robert N. Butler in 1969. According to Alex Comfort in his 1976 book, *Age Prejudice in America*, ageism is a dislike of aging and a dislike of older people based on the belief that aging makes people unattractive, asexual, unemployable, unintelligent and mentally incompetent.

Ageism is a double-edged sword. It limits how people are perceived in our society, dictating what they can and cannot do or become and unfortunately, people internalize it as they grow older. Make no mistake: we begin to define our lives by the ageist attitudes hammered into us by society at a *very* early age.

Do you really think that as you grow older you become less of who you are and more like those popular images of aging? Less intelligent, less capable and less sexual? We need new images of aging that challenge us to be excited about what life has to offer. But in order to move forward with clarity we must know the truth about growing older.

I especially want this book to enlighten a whole generation: those born between 1946 and 1964—the boomers. We survived the 60s, endured the 70s, persisted through the 80s, succeeded in the 90s, and we should blossom in the 2000s. Thankfully, I am growing older by the minute but I do not want to live in the narrowly defined world we have created for the "aged." I need your help. We must change the way we look at aging. We must begin to see aging as a process that flows from today and that validates who we are—not what our culture tells us we should become.

Our generation can do it. After all, forty years ago we had an entire country believing it was fashionable to wear dead raccoons on their heads a la Davy Crocket.

We have the power, how will we use it?

1

What Do You Think About Growing Older?

In Ken Dychtwald's ground breaking book, ***Age Wave: the Challenges and Opportunities of an Aging America***, he talks about the multi-billion-dollar greeting card industry and its role in reinforcing negative images of aging. Dychtwald gives the following examples from the ***Black Balloon*** collection:

(Front) ***Do not feel old. We have a friend your age...***
(Inside) ***... and on a good day he can still feed himself.***
Or:
(Front) ***You have just turned 30.***
(Inside) ***You will never have fun the rest of your life.***

This is how our culture celebrates growing older. More specifically, this is how loved ones help us celebrate our birthdays. From age 20 on, they remind us that to age is to become less than we currently are. According to our friends and family, aging is not valued as an opportunity for growth. It is about decline, depression, disease and Depends®.

So, what do you think about growing older?

Take some time to think about this question. It is important because the images that you currently hold will inform your future. They will dictate how you experience the rest of your life. Make no mistake about it: these images are powerful and controlling. They are often found just below our consciousness running over and over like a tape loop gone bad:

"Oh, I'm getting older, no wonder I forget."

"Well, of course I don't exercise. I'm old now."

"How can you think I'm sexy when I look like this?"

> *Each of us has developed a personal vision about growing older that is based on popular culture and what we think happened to people around us.*

Our images of aging come from many powerful sources: from the media to parents, grandparents and the neighbor next door. How we have been entertained and what we see on television has influenced us. Each of us has developed a personal vision about growing older that is based on popular culture and what we think happened to people around us—a grandparent who suffered through a painful and prolonged death, or a relative who became confused and forgetful. It is important to understand that our personal role models for growing older began *their* lives in the early 1900s. Their aging experience happened during a different era. According to the U.S. Census of 1920, a newborn at that time had a life expectancy of 54 years. A lot has happened since the 1920s. We have seen tremendous advancement in medical care, decreased infant mortality and improved nutrition. Consequently, a child born in 2010 has a projected life expectancy of about 78.3 years. A person who reached age 60 in 2005 can expect to live yet an additional 22.6 years—to age 82.6. We need to stop thinking about aging the way it happened to others and consider that it is already happening to us. That is why I ask the question, what do you think about aging?

A person who reached age 60 in 2005 can expect to live yet an additional 22.6 years—to age 82.6.

To help you develop a new appreciation about growing older, I have included several exercises in this guidebook to help you stop thinking about aging as a product and start thinking about life and aging as an unfolding process.

Let's take a quick journey into the future...

EXERCISE #1

Who will I be when I am older?

Please take some time right now to answer the following questions.

Step #1

Imagine yourself 10 years older than you are now.
(Close your eyes and use your imagination.)
Good. Now, answer these questions.
(Write your answers / images / catch words in the space provided.)

• How do I feel? _____

_____

• What do I look like? _____

_____

• What's important to me at this age? _____

_____

_____

_____

• Who is in my life? _____

_____

_____

_____

Step #2

Now, imagine yourself 20 years older than you are now.

• How do I feel? _____

_____

• What do I look like? _____

_____

• What's important to me at this age? _____

_____

_____

_____

• Who is in my life? _____

_____

_____

_____

Step #3

Imagine yourself 30 years older than you are now. Really. Remember in the absence of disease, you may live to over 120 years. So, close your eyes. Both of them.

Now, answer these questions.

• How do I feel? _____

_____

• What do I look like? _____

_____

• What's important to me at this age? _____

_____

_____

_____

• Who is in my life? _____

_____

_____

_____

Feel free to take this out as many years as you would like and examine your feelings as you do it.

I am constantly amazed at the responses people have in doing this exercise as they "suddenly" grow older. Some really enjoy it, while others simply cannot imagine themselves aging at all. In fact, they can't even close their eyes after they picture themselves 10 years older than they currently are. The looks on their faces and their comments reveal that growing older is, for them, too frightening to imagine. The "Great Unknown"—or rather what they think might be out there—may bring decline, decrepitude, depression and death. Sounds scary, doesn't it?

Now, review your answers to the questions. Be sure to ask yourself how you felt about aging at each point in time. Did your feelings change as you moved into the future? If so, how did they change? Were they more positive or more pessimistic? Why did they change? How did your looks change over time? Did you become more beautiful or more handsome, or less so?

It is not too late to change what you know about aging in general and therefore change how you feel about yourself growing older.

Here is an important question: what was important to you as you aged? Did your values change? I would imagine they did. However, the insight here is to understand what changed and why. Most importantly, were the changes imagined based on what is likely to happen to you or were they based on false images of growing older?

How you answered these questions will tell you a great deal about how you feel about aging. They will also give you a very real indication of what your experience will be like. **It is not too late to change what you know about aging in general and therefore change how you feel about yourself growing older.**

14

2

What Determines
Our Images of Aging?

Our images of aging change as our culture changes. The industrial revolution brought with it increased opportunities for production. It standardized the workday. Prior to the industrial revolution, we were farmers. When you worked the land in an agrarian-based economy you did not have regular work hours. It was said, "You owned the land and the land owned you." Your value as an older adult was tied to your land and your knowledge of how to work it to the production of crops. No nine-to-five workdays, no five-day work weeks, no paid vacations and no retirement. If you didn't farm, you didn't eat!

The concept of retirement grew out of the industrial revolution. Production and the means of production could continue without your knowledge. Someone else could learn to run the machine. With changes in the way we work and the recent rash of corporate downsizing, people are finding that decisions around retirement arrive sooner than expected. This notion of expendability carries over into how we view older adults who are retired and no longer producing according to the values of a capitalistic society. We view many older adults in our society as valueless and in fact, since they are not producing in the traditional sense, we even see them as a drain on the economy. This attitude is expressed in current discussions of the economy, social security and health care. In our culture, society casts the rapidly growing older adult population as an immediate problem, rather than an opportunity for growth. This reinforces the already existing negative images of aging.

> *In our culture, society casts the rapidly growing older adult population as an immediate problem, rather than an opportunity for growth.*

Negative Stereotyping

In 1953, Tuckman and Lorge conducted one of the first studies about attitudes of aging in the USA. They described elders as set in their ways, unproductive, a burden to their children, stubborn, grouchy, lonely, "rocking chair types," and in their second childhood.

Surely, we have come a long way from the 1950s. Aren't our images changing as our society matures? ***Not really!***

In a study from 1990, a researcher named E. Palmore found elders described as ill, impotent, ugly, declining mentally, useless, isolated, in poverty, depressed and grouchy—not much of a change from the attitudes described in 1953. Two studies, more than 27 years apart, and we still have the same negative images associated with growing older! What is going on here? Why do we have such a strong need to portray aging in this fashion? How does this imagery serve the culture? Are there hidden benefits from marginalizing an entire segment of our population? If there are, I don't see them.

Where Do We Receive Our First Information About Being Old?

Go back to your own childhood. Picture this. It's bedtime. You wash, brush your teeth, get in your pajamas and hop into bed, ready to hear your favorite bedtime story. The story probably went something like this:

Two children were walking alone in the dark woods when they came upon an old run down cottage. They hid behind a tree to see who lived there. Before long, an old woman with warts on her nose and wrinkles on her face came out to see who was there. The children hid in fear. She looked like a witch, ugly and all alone.

As young children we all heard stories like these every night from the time we were two years old. Parents and siblings filled our heads with not just ageist images: old = ugly, wrinkled, scary, warts and a bad nose—but sexist images as well: old women = evil witches. This early learning experience is quite powerful and the negative images stay with us as we grow older, feeding today's youth-focused culture and diminishing our appreciation for growth as we age.

The good news is that children's stories written today present a much-improved image of growing older. I believe this is because boomers who suddenly have an interest in creating positive images of aging are writing the stories. This is a good thing! However, we still have a long way to go.

In a study of college students' images of aging done by Barrow in 1994, students' associations of the word **"aged"** yielded the following most common responses:

Aged = old, wrinkled, gray hair, slow, less energy.
The study also asked students to respond to an open-ended question: *What are your general thoughts about the aged?* Responses included many common stereotypes about aging. See if you can spot them.

#1. "Old people are dim-witted, out of touch, plain and paranoid." (Your basic ageist stereotype, not a lot of thought put into it.)

#2. "I think we must take care of our aged and provide good care for them. We must not treat them as a burden to society."

According to Barrow, this last is an example of a *compassionate stereotype.* Compassionate stereotypes show some positive qualities. "We must take care of our aged" but "we must not treat them as a burden to society." The sentiment is honorable but the images are horrible, implying that all old people need to be taken care of and are therefore a burden.

#3. "They are the wise ones, their wisdom and life experience should not go unnoticed. They should not simply be put into nursing homes and forgotten."

In this example, Barrow talks about the double-bind stereotype. Older people can be seen as wise but we still have the ever-present stereotype of all old people being sick and abandoned in a nursing home.

Do we have any positive images of aging? Of course we do. In Barrows' study, the college students' positive associations to the general thoughts about aging were: "Wise, well-to-do, kind, patient, generous, loving and friendly." There we go. Now we have it. All old people are wise, generous and loving. Numerous times after mentioning that I work with with older adults, people reply that they, too, just *love* the elderly. To which I ask, "*ALL* of the elderly? Have you met my neighbor?"

The attitudes expressed in stories about aging are both right and wrong. Some older adults are sick and frail, others are robust and active. Some are friendly, spontaneous and fun to be around—others most certainly are not. It is important to understand that older adults are not all alike. They do not make up a homogeneous group. Nothing about growing older makes you lose your individuality. Think about some people you have known for a long time. Have they really changed that much since you first met them? Chances are they have faced many of the challenges we all face as we grow, but they did so on their own terms. They reacted to life by doing what they do best, which is what generally works for them.

> *Try to be aware of the words and images you use when you speak about aging. Do they reflect reality or are they reflections of our early learning?*

Berneice Neugarten from the University of Chicago has been researching and writing in the field of aging for many years. Her research has shown that a group of 17-year-olds are much more alike than a group of 70-year-olds. This makes sense. The 17-year-olds have only been alive for 17 years, and have probably only been paying attention for four or so of those years. A group of 70-year-olds, on the other hand, has experienced all that has transpired in our society over the last 70 years: the birth and growth of TV, computers, cell phones and space travel—just to mention a few of the technological advancements of our age.

Their lives are much more diverse and their experiences much more varied—yet, we continue to try to stereotype individuals in this rapidly changing group. We continue to try to homogenize their life experiences so we can understand them. As if just by virtue of their age, they are so very different from us. The reality is that they are you and I, just older.

Try to be aware of the words and images you use when you speak about aging. Do they reflect reality or are they reflections of our early learning? Also, please do not send people you love birthday cards that prey upon their fears of aging. These cards are ageist, and because people who love us send them, they are very powerful. The next time you want to celebrate a birthday, tell the person you love them—that you are glad they are in your life. Do not underestimate the power of receiving cards with negative images of aging year after year after year. They do indeed reinforce our fears.

There are other cards out there (funny ones) that don't chip away at a person as they age, such as the one I received on my last birthday:

(Cover)
Brother-in-law, on your birthday,
I thought I'd tell you how I feel....
(Inside)
I feel fine!

To replace our negative images of aging with realistic expectations will take work. Ageism, like sexism and racism, is deeply ingrained. Racists and sexists however, are not

21

likely to become objects of their own ignorant oppression. But the person who perpetuates ageism will eventually pay a personal price. With any kind of luck, they will grow into the narrow world they created with their negative images of aging.

3

The Myths of Aging Revealed

In the previous chapter, we talked about how we developed the fear of aging and what we are doing to perpetuate the myths. In this chapter I want to get to the heart of the matter and address some of the common myths of aging, contrasting myth with fact.

First, let's test your myth/fact orientation. We will use E. Palmore's *Facts of Aging* questionnaire, a short test used to introduce people to this subject.

The Facts of Aging Quiz

EXERCISE #2
Please answer true or false:

1. The majority of old people (past age 65) are senile, (i.e. defective in memory, disoriented or demented).

2. All five senses tend to decline with age.

3. Most old people have no interest in, or capacity for, sexual relations.

4. Lung capacity tends to decline in old age.

5. The majority of old people feel miserable most of the time.

6. Physical strength tends to decline in old age.

7. At least one-tenth of the aged are living in long-stay institutions.

8. Aged drivers have fewer accidents per person than do drivers under age 65.

9. Most older workers cannot work as effectively as younger workers.

10. About 80% of the aged are healthy enough to carry out normal activities.

11. Old people are set in their ways and unable to change.

12. Old people usually take longer to learn something new.

13. The reaction time of most old people tends to be slower than the reaction time of younger people.

14. In general, most old people are alike.

15. The majority of old people are socially isolated and lonely.

16. Most medical practitioners give low priority to the aged.

17. The majority of older people have incomes below the poverty level *(as defined by the Federal Government)*.

18. Older people become more religious as they age.

How do you think you did?

Here are the answers.

1. The majority of old people (past age 65) are senile, (i.e. defective memory, disoriented or demented). **False** According to Raskind and Peskind (1992), only 4 to 8% of the population age 65+ has symptoms of dementia (typified by mental confusion, loss of memory, incoherent speech, and poor orientation to the environment) that are significant enough to impair their ability to live independently. It is true that dementia tends to become more of a concern as one ages. At age 85+ close to 37% experience some difficulty. However, the general notion that all older people are forgetful is a myth. I hear people who forget something say, "Oh, I just had a senior moment." This is said to cover for forgetting something and the attendant fear that others will see it as a sign of getting old. The reality is that all of us forget things from time to time. Forgetting is natural. But those of us who are younger do not feel the pressure to cover up. Heck, not only did I lose my car keys one time when I was younger. I lost my whole car for a weekend and it wasn't because of a senior moment!

2. All five senses tend to decline with age. **True**

All five senses do tend to decline with age. Think about it. Vision, hearing, taste, smell and touch are very important parts of how we receive and process information. With a decline in the senses, older adults usually adjust what they are doing: turn the TV up, put more salt or seasoning on the food, install 100-watt bulbs in the bathroom. This is also why some older drivers move more slowly than other drivers would like. But if they are driving as safely as they feel they should, do we really need to get on their bumper and blow the horn? Do we really want them to drive faster when they do not feel in control? How much time are we really losing when we allow older drivers to set their own pace? Relax. Listen to the music, smell the coffee. In fact, stop for coffee. You probably will not be any further behind.

3. Most old people have no interest in or capacity for sexual relations. **False**

This question addresses the myth of the asexual older adult. Of course it is false. Studies find that adults in their 70s and 80s report being sexually active. I often ask this question in presentations and invariably people believe it is true. I ask them one simple question: When do you plan on stopping? When do you think sexual contact or the need for loving touch will be unimportant to you? They usually turn a deep shade of red but they get the point. For more information on sexuality and growing older skip to Chapter 8 (unless, of course, curiosity got the best of you and you skipped to that chapter first!)

4.   Lung capacity tends to decline in old age. True
The lungs lose their elasticity and they require more effort to expand and fully contract. According to Hooyman and Kiyak, "vital capacity," or the maximum amount of oxygen that is brought into the lungs with a deep breath, declines. They further state that a man in his 70s inhales three quarts of air compared with a young man of age 25 drawing in six quarts.

5.   The majority of old people feel miserable most of the time. False
The American Association of Retired Persons' (AARP) research shows that when surveyed, older adults say they are very happy, thank you.

6.   Physical strength tends to decline in old age. True
Muscle strength (endurance) and muscle power (explosive power) both decline with age beginning in the 30s. Of course, with regular use, these changes can be slowed. Research from Tufts University shows that if you exercise you can improve your abilities at any age.

7.   At least one-tenth of the aged are living in long-term care facilities. False
The reality is that only 5 to 7% of older adults need the assistance of long-term care. Currently, 80% of all older adults are healthy and able to live alone without assistance. But that is not the popular image. Most people believe that growing older means nursing home care.

8. Aged drivers have fewer accidents per person than drivers under the age of 65 do. **True**

> *Remember, although there are physical changes that occur as we age, people tend to adapt to these changes and minimize their limitations.*

Drivers over the age of 65 have fewer accidents per person that those under the age of 30. A study conducted in 1988 found that fatalities per million rose slightly for people age 70+. Still they were less than half of those experienced by younger drivers. Remember, although physical changes occur as we age, people tend to adapt to these changes and minimize their limitations.

9. Most older workers cannot work as effectively as younger workers. **False**
Older workers are a true resource. Economic studies of older workers show that they make fewer mistakes, are sick less often and tend to stay with the company longer than younger workers do.

10. About 80% of the aged are healthy enough to carry out their normal activities. **True**
Census reports show that 80% of older adults report they are living independently.

11. Old people are set in their ways and unable to change. **False**

Older adults are a vital part of our economy because they *do* change—they try new products and services. The catch is that they are not likely to change on a whim. There has to be a perceived advantage for them to make a change. A good example of this is the ATM debate. Banks would like us all to use ATMs for our transactions because it saves them money on personnel. However, banks find it difficult to get many older customers to use ATM machines. Some conclude that older adults cannot understand the machines and will not learn to use them. What the banks fail to realize is that in retirement, time is often not as much of an issue and older adults generally like to entrust their money to people whom they can hold personally responsible rather than a machine. This is particularly true for the current generation of older adults who have in one way or another lived through the Great Depression. In the ATM case, learning something new is not the issue. Changing the older consumer's behavior is frustrating because individual service outweighs any claims of saving time or convenience.

12. Old people usually take longer to learn something new. **True**

According to Robert Atchley, "All studies of performance show a decline in learning with age." With changes in the senses, decreased oxygen consumption and a lifetime of experience to check out, it is natural that any new information is processed at a slower rate. Older adults may have 60 to 70 years' worth of information to check the new information against. This does not mean that as we age we cannot learn new things. It just means if we think it is worth knowing, we check it out before committing it to the hard drive.

13. **The reaction time of most old people tends to be slower than the reaction time of younger people. True**
However, if you continue to exercise a function such as typing, you will see less of a decline. In fact, for people who have been couch potatoes and begin to exercise later in life, they will actually improve reaction time as well as muscle strength and endurance. The phrase "use it or lose it" very much applies to the process of aging.

14. In general, most old people are pretty much alike. False
This is another great myth of aging. It assumes that as you age and experience all that life has to offer, instead of cultivating your sense of self, you take on the attributes of your peer group. As you age, you become more like others and less of an individual. This is, of course, wrong. Carl Rogers, a humanist psychologist and the author of ***On Becoming,*** writes about refining our concept of self as we experience more of life. In fact, as we age we become more like ourselves and less like anyone else.

15. **The majority of old people are socially isolated and lonely. False**
The majority of older adults do not feel that they are isolated. They may be alone if they are widowed or never married, but they are not necessarily lonely.

16. **Most medical practitioners give low priority to the aged. True**

While this is changing as we grow older, I am sad to say that it is true. Medical education and medical students have had their images of aging shaped by ageism. How could they not? It is not uncommon to hear medical practitioners talk about wanting to work with the young, helping people experience life, believing that work with older adults is about death and decline.

17. **The majority of older people have incomes below the poverty level** *(as defined by the Federal Government.)* **False**

This is actually an old myth, although still in play. It says that all older people are poor and are a drain on social resources. The new myth is that all older people are rich, greedy and will not give anything to anybody. The reality is that close to 25% of all older adults live at or below poverty level. The majority of this group, with the help of Social Security, exists just above official poverty standards. The older population mirrors our general population with a growing division between the haves and the have-nots. The other reality is that the health, education and economic status of the older population are improving and will continue to improve.

18. Older people become more religious as they age. False

Yes, false. Studies have shown that older adults do become more and more spiritual as they age. But participation in organized religious institutions declines.

Myth vs. Reality

Now you know the answers. What a great time you can have at your next party! When things get a little slow, just have everybody take the *Facts of Aging Quiz.* You can even pretend that you are Alex Trebec on *Jeopardy;* you, too, have all the answers. I guarantee that people will be talking about your party for years to come. Of course, being unenlightened, they may never come to another party at your house. You can always say that they just have difficulty learning new things.

4

Aging vs. Illness

What do you expect? You're getting older!

Too often friends, family and even personal physicians regard this statement as insightful when it is actually ignorant. If your physician has said this to you, my advice is "run, don't walk" to another doctor who has the time and knowledge to care for you.

Here is a popular joke that says it all:

Doctor to Jake, an 80-year-old gentleman from "down Maine": "So what brings you in here, young man?"

Jake: "My right knee is really hurting me, Doc!"

The doctor performs a quick blood pressure exam and says, "Well Jake, you're 80 years old, you've got to expect these things."

Jake responds, "Well Doc, near as I can tell, my left knee is 80 years old too, and it feels fine."

We are told that one thing or another is to be expected as a normal part of aging when in reality it is not. You may be living with a problem that can be corrected. This is why it is so important to understand what "normal aging" is and what it is not. Everyone experiences the process of aging differently, so it is important to address any concerns we have for ourselves or a loved one with a qualified physician, preferably a geriatrician.

> *Everyone experiences the process of aging differently, so it is important to address any concerns we have for ourselves or a loved one with a qualified physician, preferably a geriatrician.*

A geriatrician is a physician who specializes in the care and treatment of older adults in the same way that a pediatrician cares for children. The term "geriatrician" may be new to you. Trust me, you can find one, but you may have to do some searching. Our medical schools are just now beginning to produce medical practitioners who specialize in the field of geriatrics. Until recently it has not been a fashionable specialization. But while we wait for the medical field to catch up we must be able to tell if something is a "normal part of aging" or is illness.

A researcher named Strehler suggests the following as a quick guideline to determine if something is a "normal part" of aging:

Three Conditions Have to Be Met to Have Something Considered Biological Aging.

1. To be a part of the aging process, a phenomenon must be universal.
It must happen to everyone. For example, while the likelihood of getting cancer increases as we age, not all older people get cancer. So, you cannot say that cancer is a normal part of the aging experience.

2. Physical aging is an internal process.
Many factors can bring about signs of aging. Some factors are internal, but many are external. External factors, which contribute to our health or illness, include where we live, what we do for a living, how much money we make, our marital status, nutrition, exercise, etc. These affect us either positively or negatively but are outside of the body and not considered part of the biological process of aging.

3. The process must have a negative impact on the body.
The physical process of aging is characterized by decline. No book can promise to stop the aging process although many try. No magic potions exist and no amount of plastic surgery will stop us from aging. But how we age is in our control.

So what can we expect from normal biological aging? Here is a quick list of the major systems.

External Changes in the Body

Let's face the facts.

1. SKIN

The skin wrinkles due to a loss in elasticity and a thin layer of fat called subcutaneous fat just below the surface of the skin.

To test your skin's elasticity, try this simple test. Place your hand flat on the table or bed. Relax your muscles. Now pick up the skin on the back of your hand. Notice the amount of time it takes to "snap back." Younger skin will return to place immediately. The longer it takes to return, the more elasticity you have lost.

Note: If it is still up in the air by the time you read this sentence, try duct tape.

Wrinkling brings more lines around the eyes and mouth. You may also notice collections of dark pigmentation begin to appear on your skin, commonly called age or liver spots. If, however, you see changes in freckles or the emergence of very dark, black or irregular moles, have a doctor look at them to see if they could be the beginning of skin cancer.

Speaking of skin cancer, the worst thing we can do to prematurely age our skin and increase our chances of getting skin cancer is to expose our skin to too much sun. I trust you have heard this before, but have you changed your behavior?

Skin and fat also act as an insulator and a heat regulator. As we age, skin may lose the ability to regulate heat and cold, leaving us more susceptible to changes in temperature and hyperthermia or hypothermia.

2. HAIR

As we grow older, our hair begins to lose its color and turns gray. You may have noticed that it also begins to thin or just plain fall out. In fact, 65% of men go bald. Other neat things about hair: men develop coarse hair on their ears, nostrils and eyebrows. For all you women who are having a good laugh right now, don't think you get off so easily. Owing to changes in the androgen/estrogen hormone ratio, women may develop facial hair on the upper lip and chin. Isn't this something to look forward to?

3. TEETH

It used to be commonly accepted that by age 65 an estimated 50% of the older adult population would have lost all their teeth due to poor dental hygiene in younger years. As we age, saliva production decreases which also promotes tooth decay. The good news is that the use of fluoride and advances in dentistry improve the probability that we may keep our original teeth as we age.

4. POSTURE

Do you know that you can lose up to 1.5 inches as you age? As the disks in the spine shrink, so do you. Just hike up your pants...

Internal Changes

1. NERVOUS SYSTEM

Around age 60, a reduced amount of blood flows through the brain along with a decreased ability to utilize oxygen. This affects how the brain functions.

2. CARDIOVASCULAR SYSTEM

The aorta, the big artery to the heart, loses some of its elasticity and ability to pump blood as it ages. The arteries and blood vessels throughout the body also begin to lose their elasticity. This means that blood flow is reduced throughout the body.

Reduced blood flow affects:

A. The HEART

Cardiac output for a 75-year-old is 70% less than that of a 30-year-old. Blood is moved more slowly through the body as we age.

B. The RESPIRATORY SYSTEM

At age 70, people can expect an average decline in oxygen consumption of 50% compared to that of a 25-year-old. A decline in breathing capacity means a decrease in oxygen consumption. Anyone not getting enough oxygen becomes less alert, less able to make decisions clearly and feels more fatigued. *(Hooyman)*

3. The GASTROINTESTINAL SYSTEM

Digestive juices decrease as we age along with a decrease in peristaltic action (ability to move food through the intestines). These two things combined with typically low fiber diets result in—you guessed it—CONSTIPATION.

4. The KIDNEYS

The rate that blood is filtered through the kidneys decreases 50% over time. This is a concern because the kidneys filter waste in the system. This is why we must be very careful with medication and other drugs. If our system does not filter waste efficiently, toxins may build up. A good rule when beginning any new medication is to start with a low dose and build up slowly if more is indicated. Polypharmacy (taking too many drugs or taking drugs that may interfere with each other) is a big issue for older adults.

5. The URINARY SYSTEM

The bladder of an older adult has one-half the capacity of a younger person. In addition, the bladder doesn't completely empty the way it used to. Also, the urge to urinate does not kick in as promptly as in the past. As a result, the bladder gets fuller. Both of these changes mean you will probably be going to the bathroom more frequently and running faster to get there.

6. The MUSCULOSKELETAL SYSTEM

As we age, muscle mass, elasticity and muscle strength and power decrease. The difference between muscle strength and power can be seen in the following example. Holding a book out from the body for as long as we can shows us our muscle strength. Throwing the book at somebody shows our muscle power. Muscles lose their ability to work due to neglect. It does not take much to press the TV remote or surf the net. The latest scientific research says what we have always known: **USE IT OR LOSE IT.**

Aches and pains in the joints may be a result of decreased synovial fluid (fluid that lubricates the joints). Between ages 35 to 40, bones may begin to become brittle and lace-like. This loss in bone mass (osteoporosis) can make bones more susceptible to breaking, a particular concern for older women.

> *Muscles may lose their ability to work when neglected. It does not take much to press the TV remote or surf the net. The latest scientific research says what we have always known: USE IT OR LOSE IT.*

7. The IMMUNE SYSTEM

As we age, our immune system is less responsive to outside invaders. For example, the likelihood of getting pneumonia at age 60 is 6 to 7 times higher than in younger people. A less responsive immune system increases the chances of our getting sick.

8. HEARING

The older ear has difficulty hearing higher frequency sounds, making it more difficult to hear the letters and letter combinations s, f, th, etc. It also makes it more difficult to hear a woman's voice, particularly on the telephone. For some older adults, it is hard to discern the location of a single sound when there are other competing noises in the room, such as conversation or background music.

9. VISION

As eyes age, the lens thickens and allows in less light. In fact, the lens of the average 60-year-old admits about one-third as much light as a 20-year-old's. It also tends to yellow, which makes it more difficult to see certain colors such as light greens and blues. As people age, the ability to focus on near objects is challenged, which could be why your arm is cramping from having to hold this book out straight.

We started this chapter with the often heard statement, "What do you expect? You're getting older!" Well now, you know. You can expect changes. However, while some of these changes are a normal part of aging, others are the result of our environment or lifestyle. Even with the inevitable decline brought about by physical aging, we can still have a great deal of control over our aging experience by using our bodies, mind and spirit.

Staying or becoming active and fit will slow down the negative attributes of physical aging and allow us to live life on our terms.

5

Healthy Living

Earlier in this book, you read about life expectancy and life span. You were probably shocked to learn that theoretically you may live to 120 years of age! This raises the important question: What are you doing to live a healthy life until you are 80, 90 or 120 years of age? In the previous chapter, we looked at normal aging vs. illness, analyzing the difference between what is expected and what is truly an illness. We all worry about being active and healthy in later years. Well, maybe this isn't true. It's probably closer to the truth when I say, "We all worry about being sick and frail as we get older." We worry about the costs of health care, about being a burden to others and about not being able to care for ourselves. How do you think you will age? Will you be healthy in your 70s, 80s and beyond?

Here is a better question and an even better indicator of how you will experience aging from a physical perspective. Are you healthy now? If you answer this question, "Sure I'm healthy now, I guess...I don't feel sick," please read on.

In order to determine if we are healthy, we need a clear definition of health. What is your working definition of health? I hope it's not: "If I don't feel sick, I must be healthy." We have come a long way from using this definition over the past 20 years. We now understand that health is not an either/or proposition. Our health should be seen along a continuum. We understand that we can be either healthier or less healthy at any given point in time. So, what *is* a good definition for health?

> *Our health should be seen along a continuum. We understand that we can be either healthier or less healthy at any given point in time.*

Let's try the World Health Organization's definition:

> *Health is a state of physical, mental and social well-being...not merely the absence of disease.*

This is a very good definition. However, I would like to add two new important ingredients: balance and spirituality. Health would then be defined as:

> *The balance of the physical, mental, social and spiritual dimensions of your life.*

Read this definition again and ask yourself if you are healthy. Do you have balance across these dimensions, or do you tend to favor one over the others?

EXERCISE #3
Health Balance

In order to assess your health balance, rate your health along the following scales with seven being the highest and one the lowest.

Physical Health

| 1 | 2 | 3 | 4 | 5 | 6 | 7 |

Psychological Health

| 1 | 2 | 3 | 4 | 5 | 6 | 7 |

Social Health

| 1 | 2 | 3 | 4 | 5 | 6 | 7 |

Spiritual

| 1 | 2 | 3 | 4 | 5 | 6 | 7 |

How did you do? Are you in balance? Many of us are not. We tend to focus on one area and neglect or rationalize our positions on the others, believing that some dimensions are more or less important than the others. The truth is that we need balance in our lives across the dimensions. I know people who run every day. In fact, they can run from here to there and back in no time flat. But are they healthy? I don't know. I look in their eyes and they seem wound tighter than a drum. I can't tell if they're running to something or from something, but it definitely looks like it's catching up with them. I know others (self included) who haven't run in 15 or more years. In my case that was the last time someone chased me. Are we healthy? Probably not. We're out of balance within the dimensions. What we are looking for is a balanced, holistic approach. When I talk about the spiritual dimension I am taking a broad view of spirituality, including everything from formal religion to simply experiencing the beauty in everyday life, such as appreciating a glorious sunrise or the smell of the earth on a spring morning.

> *Much of what people consider illness later in life is a result of being out of balance in their earlier years.*

What do we need to do in order to be healthy in later life? The short answer is: be sure you are healthy now! Much of what people consider illness later in life is a result of being out of balance in their earlier years. The effects of chronic health problems such as high blood pressure, poor nutrition and lack of exercise are often seen in old age as stroke, sickness, confusion, and inability to perform the activities of daily living (bathing, dressing, grooming, ambulating, etc.)

Not much has really changed in the health recipe. We all know we need to eat a balanced diet. Talk with any registered dietician or nutritionist and they will tell you that if we could get the American people to eat a balanced diet of fresh fruits, vegetables, grains and protein arranged on a plate in complementary portions, at most we would need a multi-vitamin in order to ensure adequate nutrition. Other cultures seem to have this formula down. In fact, their meals consist of all of the ingredients we were just talking about. However, we don't eat like that in the U.S. We tend to fill the plate with protein and surround it with the vegetables and grains, room permitting.

I have to tell you a story. I lived on Cape Cod in Massachusetts. On the Cape the sea surrounds us, so having fish in your diet is quite common. I also travel a lot. When I go to Houston, Texas, do you think I order the fish? Of course not. I order steak! Well, the last time I was in Houston I ordered a steak and it was so big I had to have separate plates for the rice and vegetables. This thing was enormous and I was very excited! Nevertheless, I have to tell you that I had an epiphany—a bona fide epiphany! I mean, I had heard about epiphanies but I had never actually had one nor known any-

We tend to fill the plate with protein and surround it with the vegetables and grains, room permitting.

one who had experienced one. But here I was in Houston having an epiphany. It occurred halfway through the steak when I realized that I was no longer having a culinary experience. My meal had changed from a culinary experience into a competition! My body was saying, "You do not want this anymore. You are full."

But my mind was saying, "I can finish this. I'll cut it into small pieces. I'll cut it into big pieces. I'll chew fast, or I won't chew at all, but I've got to finish this!" Am I healthy? Hardly. But I am working on it every day just like millions of Americans.

> *What I am really interested in is the fact that almost all Americans know what we have to do to be healthy: eat a balanced diet and exercise regularly.*

If you're looking for the latest diet and exercise tips in this chapter, move on—they are not here. You can find them almost everywhere. Pick up any magazine at the checkout counter in the supermarket and you can read the "latest" information on how to "find a whole new you in just ten days," or turn on a radio talk show and you'll hear about the virtues of mega-vitamins, fat-blocking drugs, or the importance of eating fish and exercising regularly. There is so much information out there that I don't really feel the need to cover it. What I *am* really interested in is the fact that almost all Americans know what we have to do to be healthy: eat a balanced diet and exercise regularly. There is no shortage of information or disagreement about these facts! It's not like we were never told that an ice cream sundae was not the best choice for lunch or that skipping meals in order to be more productive at work was a pipeline to health. We know which foods are good for us. We know how to exercise. But there is something stopping us from being healthy. Let's look at the definition of health again.

Health is the balance of the physical, mental, social and spiritual dimensions of our lives.

Are there issues in these dimensions that are troubling you? Do you have or are you seeking balance across these dimensions? Are the dimensions integrated? Is there a connectedness between your social and physical selves—between your psychological sense of self and your spiritual understanding of the world?

I don't think poor health results from eating less fish. I think we are less healthy when we do not have balance in our lives. When stress and worry dominate consciousness. Maybe it's time to stop worrying and fretting about whether we're living right according to the popular press and start living a life that is real to us. We need to spend less time and energy chasing the cultural images laid before us. At the end of the day, we have to be able to tell our story and if we want to be healthy, it had better have a balanced perspective.

6

Caring For Aging Parents

When Is It My Turn?

Picture this: a soon to be retired couple is walking hand in hand on the beach. There is a golden sunset, a gentle breeze and strings are playing in the background. Imagine a golden retriever running around chasing the birds. Ah, this is the time of their lives. They are probably planning their next trip as they enjoy their "golden years." We are jealous of them and their freedom—no cares, no worries, just time to spend together.

There are two things wrong with this picture. Can you spot them? The first is that there is no such thing as the "golden years." We have been sold a bill of goods about this golden year stuff and it was an easy sell. Who doesn't want to believe that at a certain time in our lives we can relax with no responsibilities or worries? Were this true, life would indeed be golden. I am sorry to report that the golden years do not exist. Nothing about growing older entitles you to a free ride. I know at some level we all know this. When I worked in the counseling field, I cannot tell you how many older adults felt shortchanged because they just could not see the golden years. They expected life to get easier as they got older. They felt they had earned it by working hard throughout their lives. Well, the reality is that **life is work.** There are no short cuts. There is no easy way out. Your best chance of finding the golden years is to look at today and plan for tomorrow. Life brings with it responsibilities that must be met.

> *Your best chance of finding the golden years is to look at the day you had today and the one you will be working toward tomorrow.*

Let's catch back up with the couple on the beach and listen to what they're talking about.

Wife: (to Husband) "I don't think we can go away for vacation like we planned."

Husband: "Why not, we have been talking about this trip for years!"

Wife: "I know we have, but Mom isn't doing so well. In fact, I don't know if she can continue to live by herself. I think she ought to come live with us for a while. She's really failing and may not have much time left."

As society ages, these conversations occur more frequently. As people live longer, the responsibility of caring for older adults increases. It fact, we even have a term for family caregivers today. They are the "Sandwich Generation." They are trying to successfully "launch" their children from home while trying to provide care for Mom or Dad. (Note: if launch seems an especially strong term, do not blame me. It is the correct sociological term for what we commonly refer to as getting rid of the children.)

My wife and I were primary caregivers for my mother for close to four years. Although it certainly helped to be a professional in the field of aging, I still found that being a caregiver is a difficult task. It can also be one of the most rewarding times of your life as you connect/reconnect with a parent. In addition to being a caregiver, early in my career I ran a support group providing information and support to people caring for aging parents. It was a fulfilling experience for me on a personal and professional level. Caregivers echoed the statement above, saying their caregiving relationship was a blessing and a curse, often within the same 30-second period of time. Another common refrain I heard was, "I must be doing a really good job." This would pique my interest and I inquired more about the "good job" they were doing (wanting to gather all the secrets of caregiving I could accumulate). I began to see a pattern emerge. They would simply restate, "I must be doing a *really* good job." I would ask them why and they would stare at me blankly and say, "I must be doing a really good job because when Dad came to live with us they told us he had about five months to live. That was three and a half years ago."

Taking on the challenge of caregiving can often mean delaying personal dreams: travel, golf and candlelight dinners! We can feel cheated as "our time" slips away to the increased responsibilities of caregiving. Often we are left with the big question: "When is it my turn?"

How much is too much?

> *As I think back, the only real advice I gave members was to "set limits." I would ask them to imagine a point in time or a circumstance as care givers that would indicate they were in over their heads...*

I facilitated a caregiver support group for a number of years. In order to provide some structure, I would focus each session around a theme. But before I began, I would let the participants share their feelings and relate how things went since the last meeting. As you might guess, their stories were so compelling that I rarely got to my pre-selected topic. The group would identify with what was said and off they would go, taking care of each other and completely ignoring my "professional advice." Needless to say, I was always happy to let the group continue since the purpose was for members to share stories, successes and failures and to receive support for their caregiving efforts from others facing the same issues.

As I think back, the only real advice I gave members was to "set limits." I would ask them to imagine a point in time or a circumstance as caregivers that would indicate they were in over their heads or that they could not provide care any longer. This was a difficult task for the group. They were so committed to the day-to-day tasks of caregiving that they had difficulty imagining that they could not do it all. They had already provided more personal care than they thought they could; they had already provided more financial support than they thought they could; they had already provided more emotional support than the thought they could. Why couldn't they just keep giving and giving?

The reason I raised this issue is that all too often I saw members who were "burned out." Physically they were not in good shape, financially they were stretched trying to provide all the care that was needed at home. Emotionally they were drained, and socially they had stressed their marriage, lost contact with friends and had done nothing for themselves in years. Being a full-time caregiver can be likened to a lobster in a pot of water that is slowly getting hotter. You provide care day after day, year after year until one day you are cooked and you never saw it coming.

Setting a limit did not mean they had to stop their caregiving. It was meant to provide a signal as to when it was time to ask for help—to admit that they could not do it all themselves. In fact, they needed help if they were to survive as caregivers. If you are in this position, please take time to think about and discuss this with a partner. Setting limits does not limit your ability to care. It will provide you with a perspective that allows caregiving to continue, but places your health and well-being in proper perspective. After all, if you are stretched beyond your limits, who will be there to pick up the pieces?

> *...if you allow yourself to be stretched beyond your limits, who will be there to pick up the pieces?*

Some Areas to Consider When Setting Limits

- **Do you have the physical ability to provide care that may include heavy lifting?**

- **How much of yourself can you invest emotionally in the caregiving relationship?**

- **What about your partner or your children—can you be attentive to their needs as well?**

- How much intimate personal care will you feel comfortable providing when necessary?

- How much discretionary income do you have to contribute?

These are not either/or decisions. Your answers will run across a continuum and can change over time. Again, the important thing is to recognize that we all have individual limits as to what we can do and to recognize when we need help.

Where Did the Rest of the Family Go?

Another question often heard when caring for an aging parent is, "Where did the rest of my family go?" Providing primary care as a member of a family can be challenging. Family and friends have their own ideas about what you should do, whether or not they are directly involved. Most everyone promises to be there to help...*if* you need it!

When I'd talk with caregivers they would often complain that they felt they were carrying the load and that their family was nowhere to be found. Furthermore, they were providing *all* of the care and support on a daily basis and very rarely got even an "atta boy!" for their efforts from Mom or Dad. But when a sibling would come to visit for even an hour or two, you would think they walked on water. Not enough could be said about how they brought flowers or some other gift. It just didn't seem fair to the person providing all the care while receiving none of the credit. And you know what? It's not fair. But that's often the way it is. So what are you going to do?

I would suggest that you do a number of things:

> *Let your family know that you do indeed need help and that you need them to be involved enough to know when they should step in and help— without your having to ask for it.*

1. Realize that you cannot do it all. Don't let others think they are off the hook and share no responsibilities just because you have decided to act as the primary caregiver.

2. Communicate, communicate, communicate! Let Mom and Dad know what you can do—and what you can't. Let your family know that you do indeed need help and that you need them to be involved enough to know when they should step in and help—without your having to ask. *Do* ask for help. Do *not* expect people to know how you feel or what you need. Pay attention to your own health, finances, social life and emotional well-being—and ask for help when you need a break.

Finding and Accepting Help

Okay, you have decided that you're not a superhero—you are in fact a mere mortal after all. Now what do you do?

First, congratulations for taking care of yourself. Well done! Now prepare to go where "no one has gone before," for you, my friend, are about to embark on a journey into the "where is the help I need" zone. You would think that after all of the work it took to realize that you needed help, finding that help would be easy. Ha! Not so fast! Realizing we need help and finding the help we need are two separate activities. The professional help network is a maze where we can become bogged down in rules, regulations, insurance criteria and red tape, and where you can feel like a dog chasing its own tail. Finding help will be a challenge. A good place to start is your local senior center. Nearly all communities have a senior center; all states have Area Agencies on Aging whose mission includes information and referrals.

If Mom and Dad are doing okay but need help with cleaning, grocery shopping—maybe some minimal personal care, etc.—you may want to look in the telephone book for homemaker/home health agencies. Adult day care is another invaluable place to turn for help. Adult day care programs generally run from 8am to 5pm. An adult day care program offers socialization, nutritional meals, and exercise/medication management. Some also offer nursing services, depending on whether it is an adult day health care program or simply a social day care center. An adult day care program allows you time to pursue healthful activities for yourself while Mom and Dad are in a safe place during the day.

I had the opportunity to develop and run an adult day health care program and I highly recommend them. However, there is one problem. Almost no one who needs it wants to go to an adult day care program. Family members would visit and find what they were looking for but were not sure Mom or Dad would like it. This makes sense. How many of us are thinking, "Boy, when I get older I want to go to a place every day where I don't know anyone, have to stay most of the day and play games and exercise!"?

To overcome this, I would ask the caregiver one thing. As a condition of providing care for Mom, she must agree to come to the center three days a week for two weeks. After that, she could accept or reject the idea of coming into the program. Through my experience I have found that a majority of the elders who first rejected the idea of adult day care stayed in the program once they experienced the activities and socialization. The participants would confide that, "they liked helping out the other people who were less fortunate than themselves." The caregivers were pleased because instead of Mom sitting in a chair watching television all day, she would be out of the house having fun. In fact, they often reported that Mom was much more talkative than she had been. One of the reasons for this is that she now had her own life outside the family and she was more engaged. The

> *Almost no one who needs it wants to go to an adult day care program.*

caregivers were also feeling better about themselves because they had a chance to take care of themselves and their business knowing that Mom (or Dad) was in a good place.

Summary: Give Yourself Credit!

Agreeing to take on the role of caregiver can be a difficult task. You are taking on something that can grow into a 24-hour-per-day/seven-day-per-week obligation with no vacation or time off. But it can be a rewarding and enjoyable experience, helping a loved one get as much from their day as possible.

Caregiving is not for everyone. Not all people have that ability physically, financially, emotionally or spiritually to succeed. Before becoming a caregiver, you need to have a clear assessment of the task, how much care will be required, and what type of care is needed: personal care, financial support, meal preparation, etc. Do I have a relationship with the person needing the care that will allow us to have a positive experience? Do I have the support of my family? How will this relationship change as we move deeper into the role of caregiving? Taking on this task without being honest with your partners or yourself can lead to disastrous consequences for all concerned.

In a way, it all goes back to knowing your limits. Are you capable of being a caregiver or could you be of greater help being a care manager, assessing what is needed and finding help? Research shows that there is a distinction between males and females as to their role in caregiving. Women tend to assess the situation and then ask,"Okay, what do I need to do?" while men assess the same situation and ask, "Okay, who do I need to call?" As far as I am concerned, both of these approaches are valid.

7

Retirement:
It's Not What You Think It Is!

I was traveling across country one day, reading a book and minding my own business, when the person sitting next to me asked where I was going. I told him that I would soon be delivering a two-day session in New York focusing on pre-retirement planning. He was so excited. I guessed that he was approaching "retirement age" and my suspicions were confirmed as he asked, "How much money do you think I need to retire?" This is usually the first—and most often only—question people ask when they think about retiring. How much am I going to need?

I told him I couldn't answer that question as I only handled the life management portion of the seminar and someone else addressed the financial aspects of retirement. I suppose the interview committee might have chosen me to address both had it not been for my response to their asking, "What is your financial planning philosophy?" To which I replied, "My financial planning philosophy? I've got one... and I am going to tell you just what it is...in just a second."

Then after quick deliberation I stated, "I think on the day you die you ought to bounce a check!" I was proud of this answer and they said to me, "With an answer like that, we will have you handle the life management part of our seminars; we're not going to let you **near** the numbers with that attitude."

I thought that this might dissuade my cabin mate, but it didn't stop him. He simply said, "Oh, but how much do you think I need, really?" I could tell that he was not going to take "I don't know" for an answer since, in a nice way, I had just tried that. So I told him that the answer to his question was really dependent upon individuals and their circumstances—that how much people need varies dependent upon their hopes, dreams and aspirations for the future. With that, I returned to my book, certain I had given him a good answer. But, no! He asked again, "No, **really.** What do you think a person my age would need to retire successfully?" I said, "Oh, retire **successfully!** Well then, that will take about (pause for effect with a look straight in the eye) about $1.5 million dollars." With that, his jaw dropped and he stared straight ahead for the rest of the flight.

Now, you need to know that the $1.5 million dollars was a number pulled out of thin air so that I could get back to my book. He seemed a rather insistent person and I didn't want to have to do the whole seminar for him on the plane. However, part of the answer I gave him was true. It does depend on individual circumstances, lifestyles and goals for the future. As a rule, the financial wizards I have the privilege to work with report that people should strive to receive about 80% of their current income in retirement if they intend to maintain their current lifestyles.

In order to do this, fellow boomers, I hate to say it, but we must **SAVE!** There. I said it. It's out in the open. **We must save and invest for the future.** This is something our generation is not doing well.

Living in the moment is a good thing! However, living under the bridge is generally not. We must save and invest for the future. The good news is that there are many more vehicles for investing than there have been in the past. Traditionally, we worked for a company that provided retirement pay based upon years of service.

> *I hate to say it, but we must SAVE! There. I said it. It's out in the open. We must save and invest for the future.*

This did two things: (1) it provided us with income in retirement and (2) it kept us at the company for most of our lives. We were trapped. We could not leave or we would forfeit retirement income. Now, of course, the work environment is changing on a daily basis. We have the ability to make our retirement savings more portable than in previous generations. That is the good news. The bad news is that many boomers do not think of funding their retirement until they are about 5 to 10 years from when they would like to retire. Then they want to develop an investment plan that will provide huge returns with very little risk, so they can be set in the future. Yeah, and I always wanted to be one of the Beatles.

> *Solid financial planning requires a long view. Money invested over time generally provides a solid return. It is the long view that yields the greatest return on investment.*

Solid financial planning requires a long view. Money invested over time generally provides a solid return. It is the long view that yields the greatest return on investment. "The long view!" Boomers are not generally considered the long view generation. We are better known for wanting it **now!** The funny thing is, for the most part this attitude has worked, or we wouldn't still be using it. However, when it comes to investing, we need to adopt a different mind set. The long view. This means that we have to deny our inclination to buy the latest and greatest electronic equipment and instead invest the money in a fund that will give us a return in 20 or 30 years!

Retirement

While we are talking about 20 to 30 years, let's talk about retirement. The very idea of retirement is changing right before our eyes. Let me ask you a question. When a person retired in the 1920s or 1930s, how many years on average did they spend in retirement? If you answered about seven years, you were correct! Back then, all that was thought about retirement was recreation and leisure.

When I first got into the field of aging, it was common to ask someone what they were going to do in retirement.

Me: What are your plans for retirement?
Respondent: Well, my wife and I thought we would rent an RV and drive around the country and then...I don't know...die!

To this I'd say:
Me: Well, that sounds like a good idea. Drive slow!

It was easy back then. All we were talking about was recreation and leisure. The question was how were you planning to fill out the last six or seven years of your life.

Now, because people are living 10, 20, 30, even 40 years or more into their retirement years, we are finding that the previous notion of retirement just does not fit. We wish that it did. It sounded like a swell time. For many of us, retirement has been on our minds since the first day we started work—when can I retire and goof off all day long? While this is a great delusion, the reality of market volatility and its impact on retirement portfolios, combined with increasing life expectancy, means that we just may be working a little longer than we had previously thought.

> *Today, retirement is not about recreation and leisure. It is about bringing meaning to the last third of our lives.*

Today, retirement is not about recreation and leisure. It is about bringing meaning to the last third of our lives. The question is not how much golf I can play, it is what I am going to do with my time that brings value to my life—and while we're at it, how about if it brings a little more money to my savings.

A trend is emerging that has retirees going back to school, involving themselves in lifelong learning or going back into the work force at some level. Some are going back to work full-time or perhaps starting another career. Others are working part-time, trying something different in their lives. This trend will continue.

I think this is a good thing. The old notion of retirement equaling "goofing off" has helped fuel the myth that as we age we are less capable, less viable, less...less...less. From an economic perspective, it worked for industry to encourage us to "retire" by promising a pension and a life of leisure after years of hard work. For many individuals the promise of eternal happiness after retirement was a golden vision. We even called it the "golden years." How did we ever believe that at some point in time we could put our feet up, lay back and just watch the world go by? Why did we ever think that life, at some point in time, would suddenly become easy? Think back on your life. Has it ever been easy, with nothing to think about and nothing to do? I doubt that it has. Life at any age is work. It is never easy. It always has its challenges, whether raising a family, working, putting children through college, (did I say) working or living in retirement. Life is work. This is not to say that work is a bad thing—it's not. Work challenges us to stay involved, to remain active, and to keep learning new things. This is good.

I am looking forward to how our culture adjusts to the changing face of retirement. My hope is that this change generates new roles and expectations for older adults. We know from research that when people are engaged in their surroundings—when they see that life has a purpose—they are healthier. We are living longer and, generally, healthier lives than ever before. Finding meaning in our later years is critical to individual health as well as our cultural health. The boomer generation needs to develop expectations that ask each one of us to continue to grow and develop into that marvelous work of art that we are "becoming."

8

Sex: It's Not
What It Used to Be!

Okay. Now we're getting to the good stuff. Sex! *(And for those of you who just couldn't wait and skipped to this chapter from the beginning of the book, you may move on to Chapter 9).*

After all, the guide is titled ***Sex, Drugs and Growing Old!*** It seems like we've talked a lot about growing old, and how we feel about it—how society prescribes the experience and what we can do to counter-act "ageism." Do "old people" really have sex? Let me think about it. What would that be like? At this point, many people cringe, and as my children say, "TMI!" (too much information). Or, as I recently heard on an episode of the television show *Frazier:* "Excuse me. I have to go poke out my mind's eye!"

We saw in the quick true-or-false questionnaire in the beginning of this guide that studies show adults in their 70s and 80s report being sexually active—and these surveys were done before Viagra!

The new class of impotence drugs are causing more than a few chapters on sexuality and relationships between older adults to be re-written. In fact, not only are chapters being re-written, but television advertising is getting into the swing. Whether we're being encouraged to "stay in the ball game" or seeing ourselves soaking in a tub overlooking the ocean while "waiting for the moment to be right," there are new images of aging and sexuality being developed as we speak and I, for one, am all for it!

> *...there are new images of aging and sexuality being developed as we speak and I, for one, am all for it!*

The thing that I am most happy about is that these new drugs are not sold as aphrodisiacs. Their ability to work is related to feeling physically and emotionally stimulated. The new drugs assist with an erection rather than cause one. This is much better for everyone!

As we are rewriting the books on sexual activity in later life, some questions need to be answered:

- **Sexuality, sex and intimacy: Are they all the same thing?**

- **Can you be a sexual being without "having sex"?**

- If you are having sex, does it have to be with another person or can you have sex all by yourself and still consider yourself a sexual being?

- Speaking of another person, does that person have to be of the other sex or is it okay to have sex with someone of the same sex?

- Even better yet, what if I have only had sexual relationships with the opposite sex all my life, but decide in later years that I am attracted to someone of my own sex. Can I switch?

- Can I still be considered a sexual being if I am not interested in having sexual intercourse?

The answer to all of these questions, in my opinion, is **yes.**

Yes, sexuality, intimacy and sex are related along a continuum. Humans are sexual beings with a wide variety of sexual practices, interests, and relationships. Intimacy—holding hands, a touch or a smile—plays an important part in our lives at every age. Why would we think that as we grow older we would not be sexual?

> *Humans are sexual beings with a wide variety of sexual practices, interests, and relationships.*

Of course, some physiological, psychological and social changes occur as we age that we need to understand. In addition, illnesses such as diabetes or high blood pressure, pain and some medications may have a negative impact on our interest in or ability to physically enjoy sex. If you are noticing changes, please talk with your doctor. You don't want a side effect of medication to negatively affect your sex life.

Physiological Changes

Most of the physiological changes affecting our sexual responses vary because of hormonal changes in estrogen for women and testosterone for men.

For women, changes that are common from a physical perspective include loss of skin elasticity and decreased lubrication. This can result in pain during intercourse. Of course, there are many ways to supplement your natural lubrication with over-the-counter products designed for this purpose.

What about the big "O"?

Research shows that if you were orgasmic prior to this "aging thing" happening, you will still be able to achieve orgasm into your later years. However, it may take more time and stimulation to reach orgasm and the orgasm may not be as strong as when you were younger.

For men, changes that are common include taking longer to achieve an erection. Once achieved, the erection may not be as rigid as before, and it will definitely take longer to achieve another one. Finally, ejaculation will be less pronounced.

The good news is that both men and women require more time and stimulation. So don't rush! Take your time and *enjoy!*

Psychological Issues

For women, menopause is a big event. It brings with it many issues due to hormonal changes. However, menopause is not a big issue when it comes to being sexual. In fact, when responding to research questions, many women report that their sex life has improved after menopause because of less worry about pregnancy, menstruation etc.

Probably one of the larger issues to contend with for both men and women is "body image." As we age, our bodies change. When we look in the mirror we most likely don't look like the version of ourselves that we carry in our heads. We've put some miles on and they may not have all been kind. For many of us, this realization can throw us for a loop. With each day that passes we find ourselves drifting away from that idealized version of what our culture promotes as

> *As we age, our bodies change. When we look in the mirror we most likely don't look like the version of ourselves that we carry in our heads.*

sexy. This leads many to exclaim, "How can I be considered sexy if look like this? I'm getting wrinkles in places where I didn't even think you could get them! It's a good thing eyesight changes as we get older or I'd be in real trouble!"

> *Once again, our reverence for youth gets in the way. And once again, we need to be reminded that our sexuality originates between our ears.*

Once again, our reverence for youth gets in the way. And once again, we need to be reminded that our sexuality originates between our ears. It's what we think that determines how we feel as sexual beings.

What we think about the questions I raised earlier in this chapter will lead us to our answers.

We have seen that our physiological responses can be maintained into the future. But we must use them, because like almost all physical functions, the **"use it or lose it"** principle applies.

As we age there is a shift in the sex ratio. I know what you're thinking: this could apply to the amount of times we have sex in a given week, month or year. However, that's not what I'm talking about. What I'm talking about is the actual number of men vs. women at any given age. For example in the coming years, it is expected that there will be 72 older men for every 100 older women. For the oldest-old (85+), there will be only 46 men for every 100 women. There are many factors that create this imbalance. One is that women generally outlive men by six or seven years. This affects many things like economics, marriage, couplehood and dating in later years. That is why I asked the questions in the beginning of this chapter: Can you be a sexual being if you have no partner? Can you be sexual with a member of the same sex? and, Do you have to "have" sex in order to consider yourself a sexual being?

Research shows that sexuality is an integral part of life across the lifespan. With the boomer generation leading the way, we will have an opportunity to re-define our sexual environment as we grow older.

One last thought. Earlier in the chapter I mentioned that many older women report that their sex lives are actually improving because of menopause and the declining fear of pregnancy. This is indeed good news. However, we are seeing an increase in HIV/AIDS and sexually transmitted diseases among older adults. The notion is that some older adults are having unprotected sex because they feel there is nothing to be "protected" from. This just does not fit with the reality of STDs. So the old rules of protection still apply—at *any* age!

9

Drugs and Alcohol

Prescription Medication

During the 60s, it was expected that you would share your drugs. When you are 60+ **please** don't share your medication. **It's dangerous!** I say this because it is not uncommon for one caring friend—upon hearing the physical concerns of another—to diagnose, prescribe and attempt to treat another friend's condition with "the medicine that my doctor gave me for something just like this." This is done with the advice that: "It worked for me—you try it."

Of course, the fact that one of these people weighs 189 pounds, is on no other medications and has no outstanding medical issues, while the other weighs 148 pounds and has a long list of medical concerns (in addition to taking six other medicines!), bears no relationship to the advice or medication being given.

We have already seen that, as the body ages, physical changes happen. When we are talking about medication (and with this I include alcohol), there are physical changes that directly affect the absorption and elimination of medication in and from the older body. For example, as the body ages, the renal system is less efficient at screening and eliminating toxins. As the body ages it retains less water. Drugs that dissipate through water therefore tend to reach higher levels within the system. In addition, there is less muscle and more fat. Medications that are absorbed into fat tend to remain in the body longer. Thus, dosages and side effects in our two drug users mentioned above could vary widely. Furthermore, if you are taking medications for other conditions—because of the changing physiology of an older body—their interaction may not be as readily understood.

> *It is not uncommon for older adults to experience drug interactions among the medications that they are taking.*

It is not uncommon for older adults to experience drug interactions among the medications they are taking. These side effects often look like symptoms of another illness and new medication may be prescribed for this "new" illness when in fact, it is the result of poly-pharmacy: either too many medications or dosages that are too strong. Should this occur, we might find ourselves on the "slippery slope" of drug interactions and sometimes find ourselves chasing our tails as we try to sort out what is really happening to us.

The concept that works best when prescribing medication to older adults is ***"start low and go slow."*** This means, start with a low dose of the prescribed medication and only increase it after careful observation of symptom relief and side effects. Again, because the body of an older adult responds differently from that of a younger adult, different rules apply.

OTC: Over-the-Counter Medication

A word of warning: that a medication does not require a doctor's prescription does not mean that it is not medication. In fact, given what we just discussed, it is even more important to be vigilant about over-the-counter medications—their effects, effective dosages and their interactions with other medications. For example, some common cold medicines adversely affect high blood pressure and the medicine taken to control it.

This information is particularly timely in the current age when we are being bombarded on television and in print with new medications that "other people seem to be taking and it looks like their life is better than ours." How many times have I watched these advertisements and at the end still do not know what they are for! This is ridiculous and in my opinion, shameful advertising—preying on people's fears about being sick or just plain "missing out on something." Being pushed to be the first on the block to take the "new and improved" yet unnamed medication raises keeping up with the Joneses to a whole new level. I mean, if you can't afford a new luxury car, than the least you can do is need "xyz" medication for an unspecified illness, with unspecified symptoms, that you must "ask your doctor about." What in the world is going on here? It's enough to drive a person to drink!

Alcohol

> *Speaking of drinking, alcohol is another drug that we need to keep an eye on as we age.*

Speaking of drinking, alcohol is another drug that we need to keep an eye on as we age. Remember, alcohol is water-soluble and as we age, we have less water in the body. I have seen a number of occasions where an older person is having trouble with confusion or poor nutrition and does not know that is happening. Gathering background information, I would ask about their medication and alcohol use. Quite often I would hear that their drinking has not changed in years. They just have the same two highballs that they have always had before dinner. When I asked them what they weighed when they were younger they often report that they weighed much more than they do now. This leads to the speech about body mass, body composition and renal system change.

In addition, it's a safe bet that this older person is taking more medications than when they were younger. Combining the use of alcohol with over-the-counter medication and/or prescription drugs can make for a very interesting cocktail. The results, however, are not very pretty.

Anti-Aging Medicine

I wrote about this earlier in the book, but it bears repeating. I don't care what you eat, drink or slather on your body, you are going to get older. There is a huge push to take advantage of boomers' fears about aging by introducing the latest, greatest "youth tonic." Let me repeat: "The only way to avoid getting older is to die."

There is a huge push to take advantage of boomers' fears about aging by introducing the latest, greatest "youth tonic." Let me repeat: "The only way to avoid getting older is to die."

We have discussed the importance of healthy aging and doing all that we can to forestall the inevitable decline that it brings. The secret to health is not in a pill or a potion or a procedure, no matter how much money big business spends to make us believe otherwise.

10

Rock & Roll:
Are We Having Fun Yet?

We live in a rock and roll society. Earlier in the book we talked about the importance of appreciating aging as a process and not a product—of enjoying the ride into old age whenever that may be—rather than focusing on the "outcome" of aging. I bring this up again because (1) it needs to be repeated, and (2) it relates to this chapter on rock and roll.

Due to advances in technology, we can do things that we have never done before, and we can do them faster than ever. In short, we are moving faster and faster every day. Now, I'm not anti-technology. I know that technology can be very beneficial. It's just that I do not want to measure my life by the number of things I have checked off my list at the end of the ride, or by my collection of electronic gadgets that helped me to live more efficiently. I mean, we have computers, faxes, cell phones, you name it. We have it all—or think we have to have it all.

I want to do things that bring meaning to my life. I never want to be a multi-tasker. I know there is a big push within our society for multi-tasking. Please resist this with all of your might. People are not meant to multi-task. Computers barely multi-task (as mine is demonstrating now). Multi-tasking to me means that I now have twelve projects going and I have no idea how they are going to turn out, compared with the seven I had going before. I am not doing more things better; I am doing more things less successfully.

> *Multi-tasking to me means that now I have twelve projects going and I have no idea how they are going to turn out, compared with the seven I had going before.*

Let me ask you a question. What did you do in the car before you had a cell phone? Did you drive it? Two hands on the wheel, 10 and 2? Listen to the radio? Pretend you were a rock star, or a folk singer? You probably did. In fact, I think I remember sitting next to you at a stop light one day and I have always wanted to tell you that you put on quite a show. We have all sat in the car and sung at the top of our lungs. It felt good. It was stress reducing. And after all, we were ***cool!***

But we cannot do that now. There is no solitude in the car now that we have a cell phone. We can be reached at almost anytime and anywhere. In fact, the other day I was in a hotel room and there was a phone in the bathroom. Now I've seen them there before, but this time it dawned on me, "What do I need this for? What deal do I have to close from here?" I began to imagine the following conversation:

"Hello. Ugh, ha! Kind of busy right now! Yes, well that seems like a good mark up, ugh, ha! Well, you see I have a lot of paper here right now (looking at the toilet paper roll), but I don't have a pen. Can I call you back?" This gives a completely new meaning to the phrase, *"reach out and touch some one."* No thank you! We are not safe in the car and we are not safe in the bathroom! Is there no sanctuary left?

Where can we go to decompress, to get away from it all, to relax? Oh, yeah! The health club! There we can "spin away" our stress while we are trying to keep up with the instructor and the other members in our class. Pity the poor person who is the worst spinner in the group. For those who don't know what spinning is, picture a gerbil on a wheel and imagine that 10 to 15 others join this gerbil, each one with his or her own wheel, and their idea of fun is to see who can go the fastest and longest without falling off. Sounds great. Talk about stress reduction!

Stress was a handy thing back when we were hunters and gatherers. If I am down at the watering hole and something bigger than me is coming, fight or flight seems like an appropriate response. That is stress. However, we modern humans have taken the notion of stress to new levels. In fact we tend to make it part of our lives. You have seen people at work who are stressed. When you ask them how they're doing, they tell you they're multi-tasking out the wazoo right now—yes sir, stressed to the **max.** Then they wonder out loud, "What do you think? If I keep this up, will I get a promotion? Maybe a raise?" My answer to them is: "I think you're going to die! You can't possibly keep this up and expect to be healthy. You are literally on fire and you don't even know it!"

> *There is a saying in the field of aging that captures the reality of growing older, and it's one that I embrace. It says, "Youth is a gift of nature... but age is a work of art."*
>
> *(Stanislaw Lec)*

There is a saying in the field of aging that captures the reality of growing older, and it's one that I embrace. It says, "Youth is a gift of nature... but age is a work of art." *(Stanislaw Lec).* I have been in the field of aging for over a quarter of a century and the longer I am in the field the more I truly believe this. Youth is indeed a gift and aging, (or "living," if you still cannot get past the word "aging") is a work of art. I have come to appreciate that the aging experience is a here-and-now phenomenon. What we do with our lives at this moment matters! It is what we do with our lives now that will significantly influence our experience of aging. It is a simple fact: aging does not happen in the future, it occurs each moment we draw a breath. This is why it saddens me to see people put so much energy into "fighting" the process of aging, as if they can change it. Of course, we can improve our health and vitality and this is a reasonable goal. We will feel better, be able to enjoy the moment and be up for the challenge of living. However, it is a waste of precious energy to put so much effort into fighting something that is going to happen naturally. We will, with any kind of luck, become old.

There is another term that has great meaning for me. It is *"conscious use of self."* Conscious use of self, to me, means doing the work to understand who you are—your values, what is important to you and what you expect from your self and others. The "new age" way of saying it is to "stay present in the moment." While

> *...it is a waste of precious energy to put so much effort into fighting something that is going to happen naturally. We will, with any kind of luck, become old.*

staying present in the moment is certainly an ingredient of conscious use of self, it is only a part of it. ***Conscious use of self*** takes a lot of work.

> *Our culture rewards individuals who work, but it does not want people going around thinking about themselves.*

Our culture rewards individuals who work, but it does not want people going around thinking about themselves. That, according to the messages we receive, is selfish. We want you to work and produce, and if you could only work and produce a little more, that would be just great. If you do that enough, we will let you buy things. I guess the idea is, if you buy enough things, you will know who you are. Furthermore, if you buy enough stuff with big labels on them, your neighbors will know who you are too. So don't worry about yourself, just work. Now the things that we can buy are cool things—don't get me wrong—but they are definitely ***not*** who we are.

You can see how our culture works. How about our behavior? What is our first reaction when we hear that a co-worker is going on a two-day retreat? "A what? A two-day retreat? What are they going to do? Sit in the woods, hum and look for their inner child all weekend? I have better things to do than that! I have to mow the lawn and wash the car this weekend—you know...important stuff. I would never waste time thinking about myself."

When you think about it, the person going on the retreat is most likely saying, "I'd like to spend two days trying to figure out my purpose on this planet!" They're not trying to figure out what they need to do next. We all have long "to-do" lists that we check off every day. But, in life's big picture, why are we here?

> *We all have long "to-do" lists that we check off every day. But, in life's big picture, why are we here?*

This idea of youth as a gift and aging as a work of art works on many levels. It challenges us to invest in our future at a very personal level. When I consider myself a work of art in progress, then what I do—including my work, who I associate with, and, in short, how I conduct my life—will all be done to improve the work of art that I am trying to become.

Secondly, it places an emphasis on the present. There is no guarantee that tomorrow will ever come. Too many times I have spoken with people who are not having fun now, but they plan to have a great time when they retire. The sad part of this story is that if you don't know how to or won't let yourself have fun now, how do you think you will be able to do this in the future? All too often, dreams pushed off into the future manage to remain just out of reach. Or to quote Langston Hughes, **"What happens to a dream deferred, it dies like a raisin in the sun."**

Thirdly, adopting **conscious use of self** as a way of understanding our place in the world helps us fight racism, sexism and ageism. While the culture is busy telling us what we can or cannot be as we grow older, if we have a solid sense of self, we are more inclined to answer back, "Oh yeah, that's interesting, but I have my own plan. So I'm not so sure that applies to me. This is **my** life we're taking about."

I do not mean to imply that ageism, racism or sexism can be that easily dismissed. It cannot. However, I do believe that if we are taught—at **any** age—that each of us is important; that our lives matter; that who we are becoming is to be cherished, then a lot of the misinformation our culture puts out about racism, sexism and the aging experience will be less harmful.

If we can appreciate and hold our lives as works of art in progress, then my guess is that we just might be able to appreciate the work of art in others. Perhaps then, we will be able to more clearly identify those things that we share as inhabitants of this planet and be able to move away from a value system that separates us from one another. No matter what our age, we all have a need to feel valued and connected.

11

Developing a Personal Action Plan: *You* Are in Charge!

My life as a work of art? That's a lot of pressure! I mean, I'm so busy that, frankly, I'm happy if I can make it through the day! It sounds good, but how do I get from "life in the fast lane" to creating a work of art?

This is a good question and I do not have the answer for you, although I heard a quote the other day that may have a piece of the answer in it. The quote was: "The trouble with living life in the fast lane is that you get to the other end in an awful hurry." *(John Jensen)*. I don't know about you, but this is one race that I don't want to finish first!

Perhaps it's time to slow down just a bit and reflect on your journey instead of racing to the next "marker of success."

I have offered a few different exercises in this guide. First, there was the *"Who Will I Be When I Am Older"* exercise—an opportunity to look at your own attitudes on aging, examining the myths that color your perspective of what it means to grow older. Secondly, there was the *"Facts of Aging Quiz,"* getting a handle on some of the reality of growing older. This was followed by a *"Health Balance"* exercise that asked: are you in balance across the physical, social, psychological and spiritual dimensions of your life?

Now it's time to put this all together.

Developing a personal action plan!

Please take a moment to answer the following:
Step #1

1. Describe who you are. Make a list of the qualities or behaviors that you believe best reflect who you are. *Tip: it would be best if you use index cards and put one thought on each card.* Make the list manageable but inclusive.

2. Now review your list to make sure that it contains everything you want to say.

3. Since who we are is very much associated with what we do (our behaviors), review the list again and separate your cards into two piles:

   1) Behaviors or qualities that you know you demonstrate on a daily basis—those you know others see these in you.

   2) Qualities or behaviors you would like others to notice but that you are not quite sure are as visible as the ones in the first pile.

Are you done? Good job. Now rest and review! Are you comfortable that you have said all that you want to say? How does this representation of yourself feel?

4. **Now the hard part!**
   Rank each pile of cards from the most important quality to least. I know this is a challenge because it asks you to make some assessments among your good qualities. Pay attention to how you feel as you prioritize your attributes. The test is: if you had to stand in front of someone or a group of people and say, this is "**ME**," would you feel comfortable with your prioritized lists. Better yet, if you are in a relationship with someone, have them take the very same cards and rank them in order as to how they see you. It will be interesting and informative, if not downright aggravating, to see yourself through others' eyes.

Now look at what you have created! I talked earlier about the notion that who you are now will be who you are as you grow older. Remember Bernice Neugarten and Carl Rogers saying that as we grow older, we become more like ourselves and less like anyone else? Do you like what your cards have to say about your future? Will you hold them like the poker players do and play the hand you currently have? Or would you like to keep some and throw others in—you know, "get a new deal"?

You can do whatever you want. From my perspective, when we are talking about *your* life, *you* are the dealer and the player. *You* are in control of the deck. How do *you* want to play the game? What do *you* want your work of art to represent? It's in *your* control!

> *We can think we are this or that, but when it comes down to it, what we do with our time is a prime representation of what we think is important in our lives.*

Step #2
Another way to look at it:
Consider this. What you do is who you are! What I mean by this is, how we spend our time on a daily basis may be a true indication of who we are. We can think we are this or that, but when it comes down to it, what we do with our time is a prime representation of what we think is important in our lives.

Try this!
1. Make a list of all the things you do in a given day: work, sleep, eat, commute, work-out etc. Make sure the list is complete and that it reflects what you do!

Next to each entry put the amount of time you spend doing these activities on a daily basis. I imagine the list is impressive, but make sure the totals add up to 24 hours in a day. (I know it often feels like we do 36 hours of stuff in a day but sorry, that's just not possible.)

2. Now, draw a big circle on a piece of paper. Assume that the circle represents twenty-four hours in any given day.

Allocate the time by dividing the circle into pieces of a pie that represent the numerical values you have on your list. For example if you sleep eight hours, one third of the pie will be allocated for that amount. If you work for eight hours, another third of the pie will be allocated for this. (If you sleep at work, you're going to have to decide how you want to allocate that time and you might want to keep your test results to yourself!) Don't worry if the picture doesn't look perfect. Just get a rough picture of how you spend your time.

When you are finished, look at what you've created. It is a picture of what you do and how you use your time. Are you happy with it? Does it reflect the values that you just outlined in step #1? Are they in there anywhere?

This exercise can be very telling. I have done this with various groups over the years and one of the comments I hear from participants is, "I've got to get another life!" They are astonished with what their pie tells them about how they spend their time. If what we do is who we are, this pie may look bleak. For many of us, it may look like...

we sleep...we eat...and we work! On the weekends, we try to slip in a little "me time" after church, chores and the football game! What a life!

12

Next Steps:
The Boomers are Back!

It's clear that, given the number of boomers nearing retirement, we are about to embark on another epic journey. This migration of boomers out of their primary work responsibilities into volunteer and or re-careering modes will take us to places we have never been before—redefining our work, careers, personal relationships, retirement, volunteering, "free time."

Will the future be unrecognizable? Will it be a new and completely different experience? I think not and here's why:

Maggie's Story

Our family has always been interested in social change, activism, and advocating for a better world. When our first child, Maggie, was about 18 years old, she came to my wife and me with a serious look on her face, stating, "I'm angry with you two!" I remember my wife and I looking at each other while I was thinking, "What's new?"

Maggie went on to explain that throughout her life she was subject to long dinner conversations about current events and standing on corners in the cold and wind while Mom and Dad held placards about a variety of issues from ending wars to women's rights to human rights to the environment, ad infinitum. She wanted to know, now that she was older and ready to chip in, where had we gone? What happened to the baby-boom generation that she had heard so much about? Why was it that now that she was older and interested, all the boomers were working too many hours, washing their cars on the weekends or driving to soccer practice instead of changing the world?

We had to admit we were stumped. Where had we gone? She was right! Somewhere along the line, our priorities were reordered! It seemed like only yesterday, but it had been a while since we had stood on the corner crusading for a good cause. In truth, we had become more preoccupied with activities around the home and trying to raise children who would ask just such questions.

After much thoughtful consideration, I gave my best reply. "Well the car needed to be washed." This, of course, was not going to fly. Maggie wanted to know how this could happen. How could the boomers of old have disappeared? I could only look at her and repeat my poor answer from above: "Things needed to be done."

Recently, I was able to send her an answer to her question that made me feel good about us boomers. Research was emerging indicating what the boomers look for as they transition into their post-career lives.

Two themes are developing. First, baby-boomers now understand that they may want or need to continue to work after they retire. Secondly, the majority of people being surveyed say that their number one criteria for returning to work or pursuing volunteer activities is to be engaged in "purposeful activity." They are defining purposeful activity as being connected within the community and helping to improve the health and welfare of its members.

I was so excited to see this that I copied some of the articles and sent them to my daughter with a headline exclaiming, "We're back!!!"

Many boomers are going back to their roots,

> *Many boomers are going back to their roots, changing the world again by using this time of their lives to help themselves and their communities.*

changing the world again by using this time of their lives to help themselves and their communities. It seems that the old proverb is right: "The more things change, the more they stay the same." We have not given up on our ideals. Perhaps our generation is just mimicking our development as individuals "becoming more of ourselves as we age."

Closing

A Personal Wish

I have spent my professional life thinking about this "aging thing." I have tried to distill over a quarter of a century of experience into this short guide and I hope it has been helpful to you. I hope you are now better informed and ready to use your energy to appreciate the process of aging, rather than trying to deny it.

My wish is that you are inspired to be the author of your unique and compelling life story—your very own, very precious work of art.

About the Author

Dennis M. Garvey, gerontologist, has had the pleasure of working with and on behalf of mature adults for over 30 years. His experience includes:

- Retirement Planning Consultant, speaking nationally to *Fortune 500* companies

- Director of Older Adult Health Services for a hospital system, including a visiting nurse association and a long-term care facility

- Dean of *Lifelong Learning* for Yavapai College, Prescott, Arizona

- Author of featured stories for *CNN, Boston Globe, AARP,* and *NPR*

- Mental Health Therapist working with older adults

The breadth of his experience is brought to bear in this "Guide to Aging," making for enjoyable, humorous, informative reading. For more information about Dennis and his work, please contact him at:

aginginsightspublishing@gmail.com

Made in the USA